BUILDING

BIG

SMART

ARCHITECTURE

by Joyce Markovics

CHERRY LAKE PRESS
cherrylakepublishing.com

CHERRY LAKE PRESS

Published in the United States of America by Cherry Lake Publishing Group
Ann Arbor, Michigan
www.cherrylakepublishing.com

Reading Adviser: Beth Walker Gambro, MS, Ed., Reading Consultant, Yorkville, IL
Content Adviser: Jeffrey Shumaker, AICP, Urban Designer, Planner, Architect, and Educator
Book Designer: Ed Morgan

Photo Credits: flickr/Rod Waddington, cover; freepik.com, title page; © Oliver Foerstner/Shutterstock, 4–5; © Nathaniel Moore/PLP Architecture, 7; © Aerovista Luchtfotografie/Shutterstock, 8; © pedrosala/Shutterstock, 9; freepik.com, 10–11; freepik.com, 12; © RossHelen/Shutterstock, 13 top; freepik.com, 14–15; © TK Kurikawa/Shutterstock, 17; Wikimedia Commons/Christopher Ohmeyer, 17 bottom; Wikimedia Commons/Hackercatxxy, 18–19; freepik.com, 20; Wikimedia Commons/Goyaforya, 21; freepik.com, 22–23; freepik.com, 24–25; freepik.com, 26–27.

Cherry Lake Press is an imprint of Cherry Lake Publishing Group.

Library of Congress Cataloging-in-Publication Data

Names: Markovics, Joyce L., author.
Title: Smart architecture / by Joyce Markovics.
Description: Ann Arbor, Michigan : Cherry Lake Publishing, [2023] | Series:
  Building big | Includes bibliographical references and index. |
  Audience: Grades 4-6
Identifiers: LCCN 2022044540 (print) | LCCN 2022044541 (ebook) | ISBN
  9781668919866 (hardcover) | ISBN 9781668920886 (paperback) | ISBN
  9781668923542 (adobe pdf) | ISBN 9781668922217 (ebook) | ISBN
  9781668926208 (epub) | ISBN 9781668924877 (kindle edition)
Subjects: LCSH: Intelligent buildings—Juvenile literature.
Classification: LCC TH6012 .M29 2023 (print) | LCC TH6012 (ebook) | DDC
  690.0285—dc23/eng/20221012
LC record available at https://lccn.loc.gov/2022044540
LC ebook record available at https://lccn.loc.gov/2022044541

Printed in the United States of America
Corporate Graphics

CONTENTS

The Smartest Building

The Edge in Amsterdam, Netherlands, is one of the smartest office buildings in the world! The building has a smartphone **app** that tracks workers from the minute they wake up until they leave the office for the day. When an employee drives up to the building, a camera connected to the app recognizes the person's car and assigns it a parking space. Then the app finds the worker a desk based on their daily schedule. Once the person sits down, the same app adjusts the light and temperature in a room based on that individual's preferences. The Edge also has ceiling panels that house high-speed internet cables as well as motion, light, **humidity**, and temperature **sensors**. The panels function like the brains of the building. They help each and every employee work comfortably and efficiently.

The Edge building is located in Amsterdam, the largest city and capital of the Netherlands.

FACT BOX

The Edge building was completed in 2015. It was designed for a financial services company called Deloitte.

In the center of the Edge is a dazzling 15-story glass **atrium**. The atrium brings the outside in. It floods the building with sunlight and allows air to **circulate**. It's also the heart of the building. The atrium is where workers gather and discuss ideas. Dutch people have a phrase for this kind of environment. They say *het nieuwe werken*, which means "a new way of working." Ron Bakker, the Edge's architect, agrees. "We're starting to notice that office space is not so much about the workspace itself; it's really about making a working community," said Bakker. About 2,500 workers share 1,000 desks to encourage **collaboration**. Other spaces offer quiet spots to make phone calls or hold meetings. Wireless chargers throughout the Edge automatically keep workers' phones charged. There are also coffee machines that remember how employees like their coffee!

FACT BOX

An architect is a person who designs buildings. Architects consider location, shape, size, materials, and other factors when designing a building.

The Edge's towering glass atrium

The Edge is also one of the greenest buildings in the world. Green buildings waste very little energy and often use **sustainable** building materials. **LED** lights installed throughout the Edge require little electricity. In addition, the office building has solar panels that collect and store the Sun's energy. The building creates more electricity than it uses! Coils in the ceiling circulate water around the building to help cool and heat it. During hot summer months, the building pumps warm water heated by the Sun to a storage area where it sits until winter. Then it's used to warm the building in cold months. The Edge also uses rainwater to flush toilets!

A grid of solar panels can be seen on the Edge's roof.

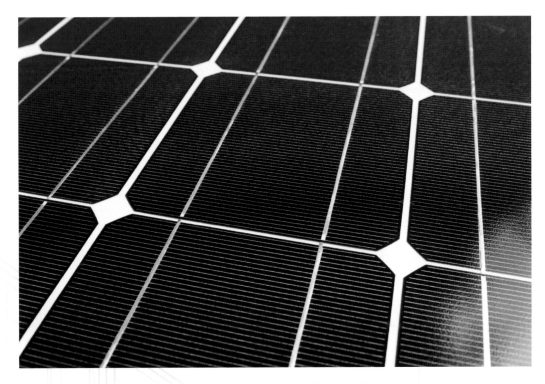

A close-up view of a solar panel

A central computer system tracks the energy use of the building and makes adjustments as needed. On days when there are fewer workers in certain areas, the system can turn down the heating, cooling, and lighting. This, in turn, saves energy. An on-site gym at the Edge harnesses the energy from a person's workout to make electricity. That's a powerful workout!

FACT BOX

Even the hand dryers in the bathrooms at the Edge are connected to the Internet. They tell cleaning people when a bathroom is dirty!

What Is Smart Architecture?

All buildings are created using architecture—a combination of art and science. Starting in the 1980s and 1990s, architects began designing buildings with smart technology. Smart technology is used to **automate** certain things. Have you ever walked into a room where the lights turn on automatically? This is an example of smart, or intelligent, technology. However, a truly smart building brings together many different systems into one Internet-based network. For instance, a smart building may have its lighting and heating, cooling, and security systems on a single IT network. This interconnection is called the Internet of Things (IoT). The network then monitors how people use these systems. And it makes adjustments based on the needs of the users. So, for example, the network can automatically adjust the temperature in a room if the room is empty. It's almost as if the building has a mind of its own!

People often use
smartphones to control and
monitor smart technology.

The first smart buildings were factories that manufactured goods, like cars. In Japan, where earthquakes are more common, architects also designed buildings with simple smart systems. They monitored the **stability** of structures before and after earthquakes. These early smart buildings were often built using heavy materials like concrete. Today, smart architecture includes everything from office buildings, hospitals, airports, and schools to places where people live. Architects now use lighter and more flexible building materials, such as certain metals and plastics, to express their vision for a building.

Whatever materials they're made from, all smart buildings use technology. In a smart house, for example, there may be smart lighting, security devices, and kitchen **appliances**. These things can be **remotely** monitored by people through apps on their phones or computers. With a simple command, smart appliances can brew coffee, preheat an oven, or check the contents of a refrigerator!

In 2007, the iPhone was launched. Smartphones helped pave the way for controlling smart home systems remotely.

Today, a growing number of architects are using smart building design. Why? For one thing, it's convenient when a building's systems are on one network. There's also added safety and security. With a smart security and alarm system, a building is better protected from theft, fire, or a gas leak, for instance. Smart systems contribute to greener living too! Most smart buildings are green buildings. For example, they may have solar panels on their roofs to create energy. Or they can turn down the heat, air conditioning, or lights when no one is home.

Many smart buildings can also adjust window shades to let in more or less light to help **conserve** energy. In addition, they may save water by controlling how often gardens are watered. Some smart buildings can also monitor air quality. They signal when the air in a room is unhealthy to breathe or when an air filter needs to be changed. Together, these things save energy and help protect people and the environment.

FACT BOX

Often, smart buildings have lower energy costs. This can make it more affordable to own a business or a home.

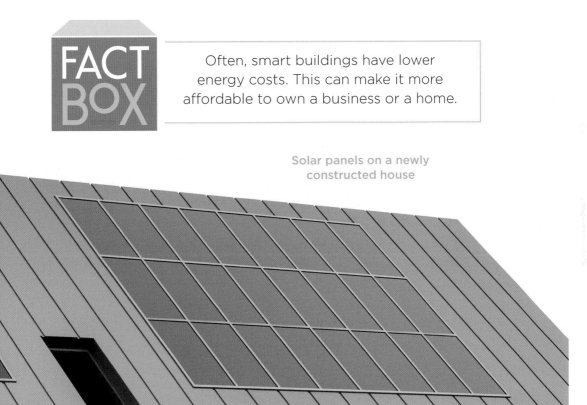

Solar panels on a newly constructed house

Smart Buildings Worldwide

There are striking examples of smart architecture around the world. The Arab World Institute in Paris, France, completed in 1987, is one of the earliest. On the southwest side of the building is a glass wall with a metal screen. The screen is covered with small squares, circles, and octagons. The shapes are not purely for decoration. They create 240 light-sensitive shutters known as *brise soleil*, a French term for "sun breaker." This architectural feature reduces heat from the Sun by **deflecting** sunlight. The building's shutters automatically open and close to control the amount of light entering the building, sort of like a camera lens. As a result, the temperature of the building is **regulated**. The building's architect, Jean Nouvel, was inspired by Arabic architecture from the past. "My job is to try and understand where the architecture will be situated, how it will be rooted, and what sense it will make where it is," said Nouvel. "A building always has links, roots."

The Arab World Institute is a culture and art center.

Architect Jean Nouvel

FACT BOX

Jean Nouvel is a famous French architect who embraces technology. In 2007, he designed a 38-story bullet-shaped smart tower in Barcelona, Spain. It received a green building award in 2011.

Another example of smart architecture is the Elbphilharmonie, or Elphi for short. It's a breathtaking concert hall in Hamburg, Germany. At first glance, it looks like a gigantic glass wave—or a sparkling crown—resting on top of a brick base. The brick base is the remains of an old warehouse! One of Elphi's smartest features is its heating, cooling, and **humidification** system. The system can adjust the temperature and humidity for the stage, seating areas, and other sections. To accomplish this, it has more than 5,000 sensors that communicate with its IT network.

That way, the temperature and humidity are just right for the audience, performers, and their instruments. Instruments, as it turns out, sound better at certain temperature and humidity levels. In addition, the concert hall is covered with 10,000 **acoustic** panels that create clear and precise sound. The panels, called "white skin," reflect sound into every part of the concert hall. Audience members say it's a magical place to hear music.

The Elbphilharmonie after it was completed in 2017

The building was built on top of this 1960s warehouse.

FACT BOX

The Elbphilharmonie is 354 feet (108 meters) tall! It's also a hotel, apartment building, and has several restaurants.

The Burj Khalifa

Far from Germany is the desert city of Dubai in the United Arab Emirates. It's where the tallest building in the world—and one of the smartest—is located! The Burj Khalifa has 162 floors and a height of 2,717 feet (828 m). The tower is supported by **reinforced** concrete that's almost 13 feet (4 m) thick. The exterior is wrapped in metal panels and more than 28,000 hand-cut glass panels. The state-of-the-art glass reflects heat to keep the Burj Khalifa cool on the inside.

Beyond that, there's an automated cooling system to further keep the building at a comfortable temperature. The system also monitors power and water use and wind speed. On a windy day, the skyscraper can sway up to 6 feet (1.8 m) in either direction. The building's base is also designed to shift in the event of an earthquake.

American architect Adrian Smith designed the Burj Khalifa.

The Burj Khalifa opened in 2010 and cost $1.5 billion to construct.

The Burj Khalifa has 57 elevators that can transport up to 10,000 people per day. Getting to the top of the building only takes about 60 seconds. The superfast elevators also act as a power source! As they move, the elevators **generate** energy, which is then used by the building. The tower also **extracts** water droplets, called condensation, from the air. The amount of water captured each year could fill up to 20 Olympic-sized swimming pools. The water is then used to **irrigate** a nearby park. The Burj Khalifa's central computer system tracks the building 24 hours a day. It identifies problems and makes adjustments to ensure the building is functioning in top form.

The Burj Khalifa's observation deck

A Smarter Future

Smart buildings and homes are becoming the way of the future. Chris, a father and homeowner in Australia, has a lot of smart technology in his house. Chris has an app that tells him when his children have been watching TV for too long. And when local weather stations indicate a rainstorm, an app also tells him what windows in his house are open.

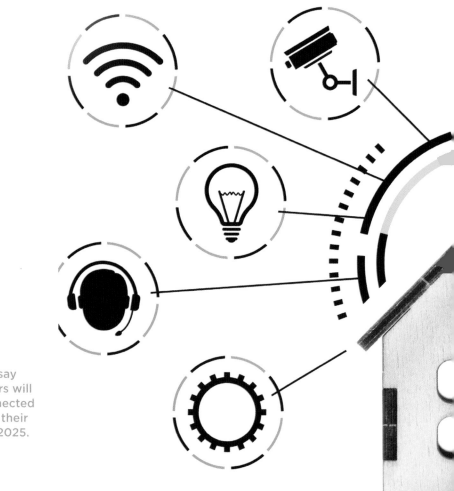

Experts say homeowners will add 10 connected devices to their homes by 2025.

And, if there's an **intruder** at his home, a hidden smart speaker makes barking noises like an angry dog. "That's some cool stuff," Chris says. His house is an extreme example of a smart home. However, more and more homes have automated systems. And they're being designed with new smart technology. Even an older home can be turned into a smart home with the installation of smart technology.

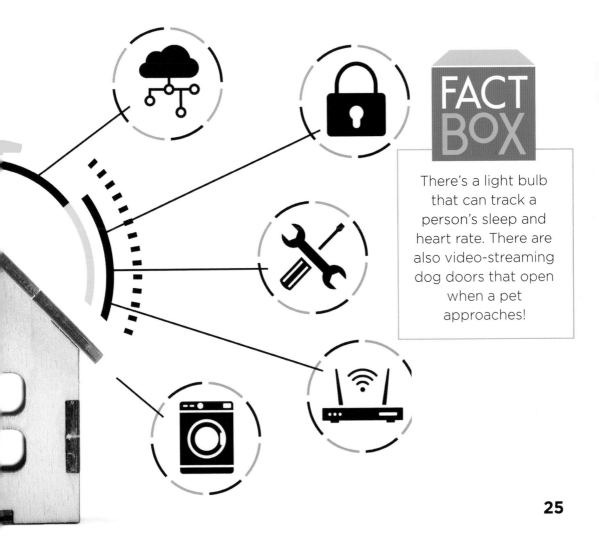

FACT BOX

There's a light bulb that can track a person's sleep and heart rate. There are also video-streaming dog doors that open when a pet approaches!

Many architects are embracing a new concept called "context awareness" when designing buildings today. This is when a space automatically adapts to the people **inhabiting** it. An example of contextual awareness would be lights that dim based on a person's mood or behavior. Another example is an alarm clock that can read a person's schedule—then set itself accordingly. Or a shower that turns on by itself and adjusts the water temperature just for you. Central to all of this would be the information collected and analyzed by the system. The home would then **evolve** to better meet the needs of the homeowners—with little involvement from them. That is truly a smart home!

Some 63 million homes in the United States use smart technology.

Design a
Smart Building

Think about what you just learned about smart architecture in this book. Now use that information to design your own smart house or other building!

DESIGN CONCEPT: What is your idea for your building? How will it harness smart technology? Where will it be located? What materials will you use to build it? Consider your building's form *and* function.

PLAN: Think about what the exterior and interior of your building will look like. How big or small will it be? What technological features will it have?

DRAW: Grab some paper and a pencil. Sketch the floor plan of your building to show the interior space. Next, draw the exterior, noting what materials will be used.

BUILD A MODEL: Use materials around your home, such as clay, paper, cardboard, scissors, straws, popsicle sticks, and glue, to build a small model of your building.

REFINE YOUR PLAN: What works about your design? What doesn't work? Make any needed changes to improve your building.

GLOSSARY

acoustic (uh-KOO-stik) relating to how well sound can be carried or heard in a room

app (AP) a software application, often a program for mobile devices like smartphones

appliances (uh-PLYE-uhnss-uhz) machines that do specific jobs, such as cooking

atrium (EY-tree-uhm) a skylit central court in a building

automate (AW-tuh-meyt) to operate with little human intervention

circulate (SUR-kyuh-leyt) to move freely in a closed system

collaboration (kuh-lab-uh-REY-shuhn) working together

conserve (kuhn-SURV) to stop something from being wasted

deflecting (di-FLEKT-ing) going in a different direction

evolve (ih-VOLV) to develop gradually

extracts (ek-STRAKTS) removes something

generate (JEN-ur-ayt) to produce

humidification (hyoo-MID-uh-fih-

humidity (hyoo-MID-uh-tee) the level of moisture in the air

inhabiting (in-HAB-it-ing) living in a place

intruder (in-TROOD-ur) someone who enters a place without permission

irrigate (ir-ih-GEYT) to use water to grow things

LED (ELL EE DEE) a light-emitting diode; a type of light that's 90 percent more efficient than a traditional light bulb

regulated (REG-yuh-late-id) controlled

reinforced (ree-in-FAWRSD) strengthened

remotely (ri-MOHT-lee) from a distance

sensors (SEN-surs) devices that detect changes in heat, light, sound, or pressure, for example, and respond to these changes

stability (stuh-BIL-ih-tee) firmly fixed

sustainable (suh-STAYN-uh-buhl) a way of living that does not use up nonrenewable resources; living in a way that can be continued forever

READ MORE

Allen, Peter. *Atlas of Amazing Architecture*. London: Cicada Books, 2021.

Armstrong, Simon. *Cool Architecture*. London: Pavilion, 2015.

Dillon, Patrick. *The Story of Buildings*. Somerville, MA: Candlewick Press, 2014.

Glancey, Jonathan. *Architecture: A Visual History*. London: DK, 2021.

Moreno, Mark. *Architecture for Kids*. Emeryville, VA: Rockridge Press, 2021.

LEARN MORE ONLINE

Architecture for Children
https://archforkids.com

Britannica Kids: Architecture
https://kids.britannica.com/students/article/architecture/272939

Center for Architecture: Architecture at Home Resources
https://www.centerforarchitecture.org/k-12/resources/

Lego Design Challenge
https://www.architects.org/uploads/BSA_LWW_LEGO_Challenge.pdf

STEAM Exercises: Kid Architecture
http://www.vancebm.com/kidArchitect/pages/steamExercises.html

INDEX

ABOUT THE AUTHOR

Joyce Markovics has written hundreds of books for young readers. She lives in a nearly 200-year-old carpenter Gothic style house along the Hudson River. Joyce would like to thank architect, designer, and city planner Jeff Shumaker for his insight and help creating this series.